MW00412187

The Underground Railroad: A Guide for Book Clubs

KATHRYN COPE

Copyright © 2016 Kathryn Cope

All rights reserved.

ISBN: 1539890384
ISBN-13: 978-1539890386

CONTENTS

INTRODUCTION

There are few things more rewarding than getting together with a group of like-minded people and discussing a good book. Book club meetings, at their best, are vibrant, passionate affairs. Each member will bring along a different perspective and ideally there will be heated debate.

A surprising number of book club members, however, report that their meetings have been a disappointment. Even though their group loved the particular book they were discussing, they could think of astonishingly little to say about it. Failing to find interesting discussion angles for a book is the single most common reason for book group discussions to fall flat. Most book groups only meet once a month and a lacklustre meeting is frustrating for everyone.

The Reading Room Book Group Guides were born out of a passion for book clubs. Packed with information, they take the hard work out of preparing for a meeting and ensure that your book group discussions never run dry. How you choose to use the guides is entirely up to you. The author biography and literary and historical context sections provide useful background information which may be interesting to share with your group at the beginning of your meeting. The all-important list of discussion questions, which will probably form the core of your meeting, can be found towards the end of this guide. To support your responses to the discussion questions, you may find it helpful to refer to the 'Themes & imagery' and 'Character' sections.

A plot synopsis is provided as an *aide-memoire* if you need to recap on the finer points of the plot. There is also a quick quiz - a fun way to test your knowledge and bring your discussion to a close. Finally, if this was a book that you particularly enjoyed, the guide concludes with a list of books similar in style or subject matter.

Be warned, this guide contains spoilers. Please do not be tempted to read it before you have read the original novel as plot surprises will be well and truly ruined.

Kathryn Cope, 2016

THE UNDERGROUND RAILROAD

One of the most eagerly anticipated novels of 2016, Colson Whitehead's *The Underground Railroad* was released a month early to meet public demand. Some of the excitement over the novel was generated by praise from celebrities. Oprah Winfrey chose it for her hugely popular Book Club while Barack Obama also recommended the novel to the American public. Whitehead's novel is much more, however, than a literary flavour-of-the-month. Literary critics have also agreed that *The Underground Railroad* is one of the most remarkable novels to tackle the legacy of American slavery since Toni Morrison's *Beloved*.

The Underground Railroad begins with a prologue recounting the story of Ajarry. Ajarry is an African woman who is kidnapped, sold into slavery and shipped to America where she is sold on repeatedly, ending her days on the Randall cotton plantation in Georgia. Years later Ajarry's daughter, Mabel, has escaped the plantation leaving her own daughter, Cora, to fend for herself. Treated as a pariah by the other slaves and raped when she reaches puberty, Cora still refuses to contemplate taking the same risk as her mother, until she is singled out by the plantation's sadistic owner as a new concubine. At this point she agrees to make a bid for freedom with Caesar, a fellow slave. With the help of underground railroad agents, Cora and Caesar begin a quest to find a state that will offer them liberty and equality. It soon becomes apparent, however, that while some American states appear more benevolent than others, each one seeks control over African Americans, from capping how much they can earn to limiting population numbers. Also threatening their quest for freedom are the slave patrollers who have the jurisdiction to search for and capture runaway slaves, even within the free states. Pursuing Cora throughout her journey is the infamous slave catcher, Arnold

Ridgeway, who, having failed to recapture Cora's mother years earlier, makes retrieving her daughter his life's mission.

One of the reasons for the buzz around this novel is the startlingly original way in which the author treats his subject matter. As Whitehead has said in interview, "I'm dealing with serious race issues, but I'm not handling them in a way that people expect." While the story is inspired by genuine nineteenth century slave narratives, it is also strongly influenced by Jonathan Swift's *Gulliver's Travels,* as well as introducing elements of magic realism. The result is a truly extraordinary mixture of realism, satire and speculative fiction. Imagine, if you can, *Twelve Years a Slave,* meets *The Adventures of Huckleberry Finn* meets *One Hundred Years of Solitude* and you might be close to the mood of Whitehead's novel. At the centre of this surreal mix is the author's concept of the underground railroad as not only a network of activists who helped runaway slaves, but also as a literal railway with a track and stations hidden underground. Whitehead then extends this fantastical idea by providing the railroad with the properties of a time machine. While everything that Cora observes on her journey is based, at least loosely, on historical events, some of the incidents covered (such as the application of eugenics and medical experimentation on African Americans) did not take place until the first half of the twentieth century. Whitehead draws attention to the slippery quality of time in his novel by introducing obvious anachronisms, such as a skyscraper erected in the middle of nineteenth century South Carolina.

The overall effect of Whitehead's curious mix of genres is to express much more than can be said in a strictly realist novel. On one level, Cora's story brilliantly conveys the emotional and physical horrors of slavery. On a wider level, her fantastical journey becomes a metaphor for the experiences of all African Americans from slavery to the present day. In describing the various forms of racism witnessed by Cora on her travels, the author highlights the way in which one form of racial oppression has simply been exchanged for another. In doing so, he creates a damning portrait of America's past and also asks some very uncomfortable questions about its present attitude to race.

COLSON WHITEHEAD

Colson Whitehead was born in 1969 and grew up in Manhattan. He was educated at private schools with a mostly white studentship. After graduating from Harvard in 1991 he worked as a freelance journalist before becoming an author.

As a novelist, Whitehead has become known for his unpredictable and experimental style which is often used to explore America's attitude towards race. His first novel, *The Intuitionist*, was published in 1999 and focuses upon the life of a female African American elevator inspector in mid-twentieth century Manhattan. Successive works have included a novel about the 'steel-driving' man of American folk lore (*John Henry Days*), a coming-of-age novel set in the 1980s (*Sag Harbor*), a post-apocalyptic zombie thriller (*Zone One*) and a book about a World Series poker player (*The Noble Hustle; Poker, Beef Jerky & Death*).

Whitehead has been a finalist for a number of prestigious literary prizes, including the Pen/ Hemingway, the National Book Critics' Circle Award, the Los Angeles Times Fiction Award and the Pulitzer Prize. In 2002 he was awarded the MacArthur Fellowship grant. Otherwise known as the 'Genius Grant', the MacArthur Fellowship is awarded to recognize an individual's "originality, insight, and potential."

Whitehead first came up with the concept for *The Underground Railroad* in 2000 but felt, at the time, that the subject of slavery was too ambitious for him to tackle. Several years later, however, he returned to the idea, which simply refused to go away. The novel's publication in 2016 was much anticipated when Oprah Winfrey selected it as a choice for 'Oprah's Book Club'.

Whitehead's reviews, essays and short stories have appeared in *The New York Times*, *The New Yorker*, *Harpers* and *Granta*. He is married to a literary agent and has two children. The author continues to live in Manhattan and teaches creative writing at several universities.

PLOT SYNOPSIS

A slave on the northern half of the Randall cotton plantation in Georgia, Cora was abandoned by her mother when she was ten or eleven. After her mother escaped the plantation, Cora was left with no one to care for her. As a result, she was banished to Hob – the accommodation where the disabled and insane live. Cora enhanced her reputation as a pariah when one of the other slaves (a respected alpha male), claimed her vegetable patch and built a dog kennel on it. Rather than give up her territory, Cora destroyed the kennel with a hatchet. After that, she was largely avoided by the male slaves until she was raped by two of them when she reached puberty.

The story begins when Cora is sixteen or seventeen (her actual birthday is unknown) and she is approached by an educated slave named Caesar. Caesar tells Cora he is planning to run away to the north and asks her to go with him. Cora refuses, unwilling to risk her life. Shortly afterwards, Cora is badly beaten after defending a child against Terrance Randall, who runs the southern half of the plantation. When Terrance's brother, James, then falls ill and dies, Terrance makes it clear to Cora that he intends to make her his concubine. Rather than give herself to him, Cora decides to go along with Caesar's plan.

Cora and Caesar escape from the plantation but soon realize that they have been followed by Cora's friend, Lovey. Reluctantly, they agree that she can accompany them. Not far into their journey, however, they are ambushed by a group of white men. Lovey is captured but Caesar escapes and Cora frees herself when she hits her young assailant over the head with a rock, leaving him for dead.

Cora and Caesar reach the house of Fletcher, a white man who has offered to help Caesar escape via the underground railroad. Fletcher tells them that Lovey was taken back to the plantation and Terrance Randall has offered an unprecedented reward for the capture of Cora and Caesar. To make matters worse, the twelve-year-old boy Cora attacked died of his injury, meaning she is now wanted for murder. Fletcher transports Caesar and Cora to the underground railroad station on the back of his wagon. Here they meet the station agent, Lumbly, before embarking on a terrifying journey on the secret railway in complete darkness.

The train transports the two runaways to South Carolina where they begin new lives. Although officially now the property of the South Carolina government, Cora and Caesar are no longer slaves. The government gives them new identities, finds them jobs, offers accommodation and even runs a literacy program. Now going under the name of Bessie Carpenter, Cora works for the Andersons, cooking, cleaning and helping with their children. After work she goes back to a dormitory that she shares with other black women, run by a white proctor, Miss Lucy. Caesar, meanwhile, works in a machine factory and meets Cora at regular socials. Sam, the young station agent for South Carolina, tells Caesar that there is another train heading further north in a few days' time. Happy with their present circumstances, however, Cora and Caesar both agree to stay longer.

One night, on the way home from a social, Cora sees a young black woman in a state of distress, screaming that her babies are being taken away. Cora assumes that the woman is reliving past trauma from her life as a slave. She asks Miss Lucy about the incident and is told that the woman, named Gertrude, has now been placed in dormitory number 40, which is reserved for the mentally ill.

Although Cora is happy working for the Andersons, Miss Lucy tells her that she has been promoted to a job in the Museum of Natural Wonders. Here Cora works as a live exhibit in the American history section. As she enacts scenes in the 'Darkest Africa', 'Life on the Slave Ship' and 'Typical Day on the Plantation' sections, Cora realises that the museum is presenting a sanitized version of history, designed to be palatable to white people. Her concerns are further raised when a doctor encourages her to be sterilized as a form of birth control - a procedure which he reveals is already being carried out on those with mental disabilities without their permission.

Cora and Caesar meet up with Sam, who warns Caesar to stay away from Red's, a local brothel specializing in black sex workers. He explains that Red's is the secret hub of a syphilis program in which black men are being infected in order to study the progress of the disease. He also tells them the state is running a sterilization program to prevent black people from outnumbering whites. Back at the dormitories, Miss Lucy puts pressure on Cora to agree to sterilization, threatening to give her up to the slave catchers if she doesn't comply. Panicking, Cora goes to see Sam who tells her that an infamous slave catcher, Arnold Ridgeway, is in the area looking for her. Sam leaves Cora on the platform of the underground railroad station under his house, while he waits upstairs for Caesar to arrive. After a long wait, Cora hears men ransacking the house above. The smell of smoke tells her that the house is on fire.

A railroad engine arrives at the station platform and the driver takes Cora to North Carolina, where that part of the track terminates. Although the station is closed, she is discovered by the station agent, Martin Wells, who has come to leave a message that he cannot accept any more passengers. On the way to his house Martin shows Cora the Freedom Trail: a tree-lined road festooned with hanging black corpses, leading all the way into town. Martin's wife, Ethel, is displeased at Cora's arrival, believing that she will bring danger to the house. The couple hide her in a small concealed nook in their attic, warning her that she must be quiet when their Irish maid is in the house.

Through a hole in the attic wall, Cora witnesses the town's 'Friday Festival' which takes place in the park. The festivities include a 'coon show' and culminate in the appearance of two night riders who drag a black girl onto the stage. The crowd of spectators rush forward to participate as the girl is hung from a tree. Later Martin explains to Cora that the people of North Carolina became frightened by the increasing black population and stories of revolts in which slaves had turned on their masters. As a solution to 'the colored question', Irish immigrants had been employed to pick cotton, while new laws were introduced to prohibit black people from living in or entering the state. Significant rewards were being offered to turn in any collaborators found aiding or hiding outlawed blacks.

After several months of living in the attic, Cora falls ill and Ethel is forced to move her to a bedroom to nurse her. Just as Cora has recovered her strength, Martin and Ethel receive an unexpected visit from the night riders, who have been tipped off by the Irish maid. The raid is observed by Ridgeway, who prevents the night riders from hanging Cora by telling them he has jurisdiction to take her back to her owner. Cora sees the crowd in the park stoning Ethel and Martin as Ridgeway takes her away.

Ridgeway, along with his colleague, Boseman, and his black driver, Homer, transport Cora and another runaway slave named Jasper through Tennessee. Here many of the towns have been devastated by a wildfire and some have been overtaken by yellow fever. Jasper continually sings hymns and Ridgeway eventually shoots him in the face to shut him up. On the journey Ridgeway informs Cora that Caesar was captured in South Carolina and, when word got out that the murderer of a white boy was in the jail, a mob broke in and ripped him to pieces. One day Ridgeway's wagon is stopped on the road by three armed black men. During a scuffle, the men shoot Boseman and then shackle Ridgeway. Homer is nowhere to be seen. After freeing Cora, the strangers invite her to travel with them.

Cora and her rescuers, Royal, Red and Justin take the underground railroad to Indiana. Here Cora happily settles on the Valentine farm where a community of black people work together for the good of all. Cora grows close to Royal and one day he shows her where the nearest branch of the underground railroad is located. In this station, the line is too narrow for an engine and disappears into a tunnel. Royal tells her that, as far as he knows, the "ghost tunnel" has never been used and no one knows when it was created.

One day Sam turns up at the farm. Having escaped capture by the men who set his house alight, he continues to work for the railroad. Sam gives Cora the good news that Terrance Randall has died and that Ridgeway and Homer have disappeared. Some of the residents of the farm are unhappy that the community give shelter to runaway slaves and its owner, John Valentine, agrees to hold a gathering where the residents will decide the matter by democratic vote. During the meeting, a white mob invades the farm and many of the residents, including Royal, are shot. The mob includes Ridgeway, who grabs Cora and instructs her to take him to the underground railroad.

Cora leads Randall to the ghost station. Taking advantage of the darkness, she wrestles with him and he hits his head on the stone steps. Cora climbs into a handcar and propels herself into the ghost tunnel. Eventually, she emerges at the mouth of a cave and accepts a lift from a black man who tells her he is heading to

Missouri and then on to California.

HISTORICAL CONTEXT

THE UNDERGROUND RAILROAD

The underground railroad was established to help African Americans escape slavery in the American South. Operating before the Civil War ended slavery in America, the railroad was at its most active between 1850 and 1860. Not a literal railway but a secret network of escape routes and safe houses, the underground railroad attracted a variety of active supporters, including free-born blacks, former slaves, American Indians, white abolitionists, philanthropists and members of the clergy. One of the railroad's most famous members was the escaped slave, Harriet Tubman, who is estimated to have helped around 300 slaves to escape from the South. Another crucial figure in the movement was William Still who is often called the Father of the Underground Railroad. Still hid a stream of runaway slaves in his Philadelphia home and kept short biographies of each one of them. These accounts were published in 1872 under the title *Underground Railroad: Authentic Narratives and First-Hand Accounts* and have done much to enrich historians' understanding of how the railroad worked.

Railway terminology was used among the railroad's members to maintain secrecy. Escape routes were known as lines and hiding places were called stations. People who helped guide slaves along their route were agents or conductors, slaves were passengers, freight, or cargo and the brave souls who hid slaves in their homes were stationmasters. If caught aiding runaways in a slave state, railroad members could be sent to prison, hanged, whipped or sometimes died at the hands of violent mobs.

The network of railroad routes passed through fourteen northern states and extended as far as the 'Promised Land' of Canada which was beyond the jurisdiction of fugitive slave hunters. 'Stations', which were often hidden in barns, under church floors or even in caves and riverbanks were generally situated between ten to twenty miles apart. Escaped slaves would usually travel by night to a station and hide there until a message could be sent to the next stationmaster along the line. Most runaways travelled by foot and escaped either individually or in small groups. Sizeable rewards were often offered by slave owners for the return of their 'property' and notices regularly appeared in southern newspapers requesting information about escaped slaves. Thanks to the Fugitive Slave Act of 1793, professional bounty hunters (known as slave catchers) had the authority to pursue fugitives, even in free states, as far as America's border with Canada. While citizens were legally obliged to comply with the slave catchers, in some parts of the North, where support of abolition was the strongest, they needed police protection to carry out their job.

Historians cannot be sure of the number of slaves who used the underground railroad but it is estimated that approximately 100,000 slaves escaped from bondage in this way. While the economic impact of these escapes was negligible (as in 1860 there were almost 4 million slaves in the South) the underground attack on the institution of slavery angered and frightened slave owners and white southerners.

THE ABUSE OF AFRICAN AMERICAN HUMAN RIGHTS

The underground railroad system is just a part of Colson Whitehead's examination of the historical experience of African Americans. While the author celebrates the courage of those who played a part in the underground railroad (both runaway slaves and helpers), he also emphasizes, through Cora's experiences in various states, that escape from slavery does not necessarily equate to freedom. Fugitive slaves who reached the free states of the North found that freedom from slavery did not mean that they would be treated as equal citizens or even as human beings. In many northern states Segregation was stringently enforced, black men did not have the right to vote and African Americans were often the victims of mob violence. A number of the human rights abuses Cora encounters on her travels are directly inspired by shameful cases in America's history.

Sterilization

When Cora realizes that the South Carolina government are enforcing sterilization on black women the scenario seems like something out of a surreal nightmare. In reality, however, this part of the story was inspired by a real American government program, forcing or coercing people of minorities to be sterilized.

As early as 1907 the American government introduced policies that gave them the right to sterilize individuals across 30 states. Initially these programs were targeted at people with defective genetic traits or who were mentally incapacitated in some way. Forced sterilization of these sectors of society inevitably led to recommendations that the criteria for these programs could be extended along race and class lines. Some states set up Eugenics Boards and in North Carolina alone over 7,600 individuals were sterilized between the 1930s and the 1970s. Notably, 65 percent of the sterilizations in North Carolina were carried out on black women even though only 25 percent of the state's female population was black.

While many women of ethnic minorities were sterilized against their will, others underwent the procedure without their knowledge. This would generally happen when the subject was already in hospital for other reasons, e.g. childbirth or an appendectomy. In Sunflower County, Mississippi, 60 percent of the state's resident black women were sterilized at the city hospital without their permission.

It is also now known that women of ethnic minorities have been coerced into sterilization by the American government without full knowledge of what the procedure entails. In 1937 a population control program was introduced in Puerto Rico. Rather than providing Puerto Rican women with access to contraception, however, the US government promoted permanent sterilization. This was encouraged through door-to-door visits by health workers, and by employers who favoured sterilized women in their selection criteria. More than a third of the women who agreed to sterilization claimed afterwards that they did not realize that this form of birth control was irreversible.

The Tuskegee Syphilis Experiment

Colson Whitehead's description of a syphilis experiment in *The Underground Railroad* deliberately draws attention to a real-life experiment which, the author feels, not enough people are aware of. Officially known as 'The Tuskegee Study of Untreated Syphilis in the Negro male', this clinical study was conducted between 1932 and 1972 by the US Public Health Service in collaboration with Tuskegee University. The initial aim of the study was to track the natural progression of untreated syphilis for six to nine months, followed by a period of treatment. When funding for the study was lost, however, it became a long-term observational study of the symptoms with no treatment offered.

600 African American sharecroppers from Macon County, Alabama, were recruited for the study on the understanding that they were participating in a free health care program. Of the participants, 399 of the men had already contracted syphilis but did not know that this was why they had been chosen for the study. In return for their participation the men received free medical care, hot meals and burial insurance. During the study they were told they were being treated for "bad blood", a catch-all term for a number of different illnesses. None of the men were specifically told that they had syphilis and none were treated with penicillin, even when it became widely recognized that the antibiotic could effectively treat the disease. When 250 of the men involved in the trial were called up for service in the Second World War, government officials intervened to ensure that the men remained part of the study instead. Ironically, if they had joined up, they would have automatically received treatment for syphilis.

The Tuskegee study continued until 1972 when a leak to the press brought it to a close. Of the original 399 men, 28 died of syphilis, 100 died of related complications, 40 of their wives contracted the disease and 19 of their children were born with congenital syphilis. In 1973 a lawsuit was filed on behalf of the study participants and their families and, the following year, a $10 million out-of-court settlement was reached. The US government also agreed to provide lifetime medical benefits and burial services to all living participants of the study.

For those who know about it, the Tuskegee Syphilis Experiment has become synonymous with unethical and racist medical research. It also contributed to a general distrust of public health programs within the black community. This distrust led to rumours in the 1980s that the American government had caused the HIV/AIDS crisis by deliberately infecting members of the black community with the virus.

The Tulsa Race Riot & the Rosewood Massacre

In *The Underground Railroad*, the destruction of the Valentine Farm and murder of its residents by a white mob echoes many historical incidents of mass racist violence. Two shocking episodes it evokes in particular are the Tulsa Race Riot and the Rosewood Massacre.

In 1921 thousands of white Americans took part in a riot in the town of Greenwood, Oklahoma. At the time, the African Americans of Greenwood in Tulsa were known to be the wealthiest black community in the nation. The area became a byword for black prosperity, leading to one of its commercial areas being dubbed 'the Negro Wall Street'. The end of the district's golden age came, however, when an African American man was accused of raping a white female elevator operator. Rumours spread through the black community that a lynch mob was waiting outside the police station for the accused. Aiming to prevent the man from being seized by an angry mob, a group of armed black men rushed to the scene where they got into a confrontation with a white crowd. As news of this confrontation spread, mob violence overtook Greenwood. Thousands of white people gathered to rampage through the area, killing black men and women, as well as looting and burning down their homes and stores. It is estimated that approximately 300 black residents of Greenwood were killed and the riot destroyed over 35 blocks of the district. Despite the horrific number of deaths involved, details of the massacre were omitted from local and state histories for many years in an apparent attempt to erase the episode from collective memory. Only in 1996 did the state commission a report to establish the facts of the massacre, acknowledge the suffering of the victims and officially commit the event to historical record.

The Rosewood Massacre took place in 1923 and involved the destruction of a black town in Levy County, Florida, and the murder of some of its residents. Before the incident Rosewood, like Valentine's farm, had been a peaceable, largely black, self-

19

sufficient community. When a white woman in a nearby town was allegedly attacked by a black drifter, however, one of the male residents of Rosewood was lynched in a revenge attack. The people of Rosewood gathered to defend themselves against further hate crimes but could not prevent a mob of several hundred white people burning down every building in the town and killing at least six of its black residents. No arrests were ever made in connection with the massacre and the town was abandoned.

LITERARY CONTEXT

Slave Narratives

During the eighteenth and nineteenth centuries, around 6,000 former slaves provided first-hand accounts of their lives under slavery. Many of these narratives were published as books or pamphlets by abolitionists, who would often also have to write down the accounts if the slaves were illiterate. Later, in the 1930s, a significant contribution to the canon of slave narratives was made when Franklin D. Roosevelt's New Deal Works Progress Administration employed writers and researchers to interview and transcribe the oral accounts of African Americans who were former slaves. More than 2,300 slave narratives were recorded during the project and the resulting collection, *Born in slavery: slave narratives from the federal writers' project, 1936-1938* was archived at the Library of Congress.

Slave narratives are hugely important from both a historical and a literary perspective. In the late eighteenth and early nineteenth centuries, they were an important tool in the antislavery movement. The accounts exposed the realities of slavery to those white people who were prepared to hear them. Reading these first-hand narratives also brought home to their readership the humanity of the voices behind them. This strengthened the case that African Americans deserved human rights and helped to turn the tide of public opinion against the institution of slavery. From a literary point-of-view, these accounts are also the main form of African American literature prior to the twentieth century.

In researching *The Underground Railroad*, Colson Whitehead familiarized himself with many of the oral histories gathered by the Works Progress Administration as well as reading more well-known slave narratives such as Harriet Jacobs' *Incidents in the Life of a Slave Girl* and *Narrative of the Life of Frederick Douglass*. As well as capturing some of the brutal details of slavery conveyed in these accounts, Whitehead also wanted to emulate their tone: "I wanted it to be like the slave narratives I read, where you get a very matter-of-fact contemplation of all these weird and horrible things that keep happening." Cora's pragmatic tone throughout the novel, even in the face of the most horrific brutality, deliberately echoes real slave narratives in which suffering becomes a daily and expected occurrence. Whitehead adds further authenticity to his neo-slave narrative by prefacing his chapters with genuine advertisements from newspapers seeking information on runaway slaves.

The Picaresque

Another influence upon the style of *The Underground Railroad* is the picaresque novel. First becoming popular in sixteenth century Spain, this genre of novel flourished in Europe during the seventeenth and eighteenth centuries and remains an influence in fiction today. Usually written in the first person, the picaresque was an early form of 'road novel'. The story would be made up of a series of loosely connected episodes in which the protagonist stops at a new place, meets new people and has some kind of adventure or close shave before moving on to the next stop in his journey. An important aspect of the picaresque hero is that, wherever he stops, he is an outsider and can therefore observe the odd behaviour of those he meets without the subjectivity of personal involvement. Picaresque narratives are therefore ideal for satirizing the hypocrisies and corruptions of society. Cora's journey on the underground railroad and her experiences in each American state mirrors the classic episodic structure of a picaresque novel. Her observations on the peculiarities of behaviour she witnesses in each of these states provide a satirical commentary upon racist and barbaric practices which the citizens perceive as the norm.

Famous examples of the picaresque include *Don Quixote* by Cervantes and Mark Twain's *The Adventures of Huckleberry Finn*. The picaresque classic that Whitehead claims influenced his novel the most, however, is *Gulliver's Travels* by the Irish writer Jonathan Swift. First published in 1726, Swift's novel is a satire on British and European society. Its protagonist, Lemuel Gulliver, travels to the imaginary countries of Lilliput, Blefuscu, Brobdingnag, Laputa and the land of the Houyhnhnms. Like Cora, as she travels from state to state, Gulliver hopes to find a utopia in each country he visits but is disappointed to find that each society is flawed in its own way. As in *The Underground Railroad*, images of cruelty and enforced subjugation abound. In Lilliput, Gulliver is captured and physically tied down by the tiny citizens while, in Brobdingnag, a farmer makes him his slave. Swift's protagonist also repeatedly observes physical force being used against others, witnessing the Houyhnhnms chaining up another species called the Yahoos, while the Laputans justify the way they forcibly keep the lower land of Bainibarbi in check by arguing that they possess superior intellect. Gulliver's increasing sense of alienation as he fails to fit into any of these societies perfectly reflects the African American experience.

Magic Realism

Magic realism is a term that was initially associated with Latin American literature and is used to describe fiction which, on the whole, portrays a recognizable and realistic world but then disrupts this realism in some way, confounding the reader's expectations. The key attribute to this genre is that weird elements to the storyline are presented as if they are nothing out of the ordinary; the magical or fantastical blends seamlessly with the everyday and mundane. Gabriel Garcia Marquez, Isabel Allende, Salman Rushdie, Toni Morrison and Angela Carter are all brilliant proponents of this style of fiction.

While Colson Whitehead strives to convey the realities of being a slave in nineteenth century America, he also deliberately disrupts this sense of historical accuracy in a number of ways. Most obviously 'unreal' is his conception of the underground railroad as a physical railway rather than a metaphor for a network of escape routes and safe houses. Until Cora and Caesar lay eyes on the underground station hidden beneath Lumbly's house, there is little to suggest that the story will stray from a realistic slave narrative. Once the magical world of the underground railroad is revealed, however, with its hint of steampunk, the author makes it clear that he is asking his readers to take an imaginative leap of faith. When Cora reaches South Carolina, another surprise lies in wait, as she is greeted by a skyscraper looming in the centre of the city. As well as this deliberate historical anachronism, Whitehead adds touches of the macabre and grotesque to his novel (e.g. the seemingly endless road of hanging corpses known as the Freedom Trail and the bizarre 'coon show'/public execution Cora witnesses from her hiding place in the attic).

Like Gabriel Garcia Marquez in *One Hundred Years of Solitude* and Toni Morrison in *Beloved*, Whitehead uses magic realism to articulate unspeakable aspects of history. Just as, in *Beloved*, the ghostly presence of a dead daughter represents the way the legacy of slavery haunts the characters, the more surreal scenes in *The Underground Railroad* underline the grotesque nature of racism. The historical anachronisms, while adding to the surreal effect, allow Whitehead to critique beyond the era of slavery to America's continuing exploitation of African Americans following abolition. Cora's journey on the underground railroad could almost be a ride in a time machine as she witnesses human rights abuses that echo true historical events from the 1920s and 1930s. Whitehead's crafty mixing of fantasy and fact-based details leaves readers wondering, on a number of occasions, which is which. Many readers, for example, might be surprised to learn that the descriptions of enforced sterilization and syphilis experimentation are not a product of the author's imagination but based upon historical fact.

THEMES & IMAGERY

THEMES

Racism

As Cora travels through different American states, Whitehead illustrates that racism isn't a single beast but can take many different forms. While every state has different laws and customs relating to race, each one sees the 'colored question' as a problem requiring a solution.

Georgia represents racism at its worst and also at its most straightforward. Here African Americans have no human rights thanks to the institution of slavery. Racist ideology is largely driven by greed, as it allows slave owners to treat their slaves like animals in order to keep the wheels of the cotton industry turning. In this slave state the main concern is how to prevent African American 'property' from escaping to freedom.

In South Carolina the racism that Cora experiences is more subtle. At first, the state government here appears far more liberal and caring. Black citizens are given 'free' status and are helped to find work and housing. Cora eventually realizes, however, that the help provided by the state is paternalistic, effectively withholding freedom while appearing to bestow it. Free status is given to blacks on the proviso that there is no danger of them ever attaining true equality. A lid is kept on black empowerment by controlling how African Americans live and how much they earn, while a eugenics program limits population numbers through sterilization. Through these insidious means of control, the state quells white fears that the African American population may one day outnumber or overpower them.

In North Carolina Cora finds that racism is just as blatant as in the slave states but has taken an even more unsettling turn. In this state, racism is driven by fear of the increasing black population and the revolts in which slaves have turned on their masters. So strong is this fear that its citizens have abandoned the profitable institution of slavery, preferring to pay Irish immigrants a meagre wage to pick cotton rather than run the risk of black retribution. In the racial ideology of North Carolina we see many of the characteristics of Nazi Germany. The entertainment laid on in the Friday Festivals consists of the kind of racist propaganda favoured by Hitler, while a form of ethnic cleansing is carried out by the night riders who scour the state for any African Americans unfortunate enough to set foot there. One of the most frightening aspects of the racism Cora witnesses in North Carolina is the mass hysteria which takes over its citizens. When a bloodthirsty mob rush forward to participate in the hanging of a black girl, and later stone Martin and Ethel Wells, it is clear that their fear of African Americans makes them capable of anything. This mixture of hatred and fear is just the kind of atmosphere in which history's greatest atrocities have taken place.

Differing degrees of racism are also represented through individual characters in the novel. While Terrance Randall represents an extreme white supremacist attitude, other characters exhibit more moderate racist attitudes which, nevertheless, are just as dangerous. Ethel Wells, for example, believes that Christian scripture confirms the inferiority of the black race and sees African Americans as savages requiring religious conversion. Meanwhile, Mrs Garner, the widow who promises to free Caesar and his family after her death, is an example of ineffectual white liberalism. Although she treats Caesar's family reasonably well while she is alive, her apparent change-of-heart over freeing them has devastating consequences. By leaving no will, she leaves their future in the hands of unsympathetic relatives who sell them on individually, breaking up the family unit. In this respect Mrs Garner represents the most prevalent form of racial prejudice. While she would never consider herself a racist, she is ultimately unwilling to go so far as to offer African Americans freedom and equality. By simple inaction she causes a great deal of harm.

Freedom

The elusive quality of freedom is a recurring theme in *The Underground Railroad*. Images of bondage and imprisonment abound in the novel (the stocks on the Randall plantation, Lumbly's collection of iron shackles, Cora's cramped attic quarters etc.) all emphasizing the way in which Cora's quest for freedom is continually thwarted. Each American state she visits limits the freedom of African Americans in a different way, from slavery to controlling fertility, to prohibiting their existence altogether.

Throughout the novel Whitehead emphasizes the irony underlying America's preoccupation with freedom. While its white citizens purport to value freedom above anything else, they have built their nation upon restricting the freedoms of American Indians and African Americans. This irony is most memorably highlighted through the story of Michael, a young slave taught to recite the Declaration of Independence. Michael becomes a celebrated novelty act on the Randall plantation, not only because he can recite the Declaration without being able to read it, but also because he was born into slavery and can have no understanding of the concept of freedom. Making a similar point, the author names an avenue lined with hanging black corpses 'the Freedom Trail.'

Property

Connected to the novel's exploration of freedom (or the lack of it) is the theme of property. The author suggests that the obtaining and keeping of property, whether it be land or another human being is, "The American imperative."

The novel emphasizes the way in which the institution of slavery makes property of African Americans. The perception of slaves as nothing more than livestock is emphasized by the branding of Cora and Sybil by their owners (Cora with an x-shaped scar from Terrance Randall's cane and Sybil with a horseshoe scorched onto her neck). In this context, Ridgeway sees his job as a slave catcher as simply returning property to its rightful owner. This notion of human bodies as commodities is elaborated upon in the section describing Dr Stevens's lucrative involvement with bodysnatching.

The treatment of African Americans as property does not end, however, with the removal of slavery. Although Cora and Caesar are no longer slaves within the boundaries of South Carolina, they are still the official property of the government. This is emphasized when it becomes clear that state officials are using the bodies of black citizens for medical research and sterilization programs without feeling that they require the owners' consent.

The ownership of property is also shown to be an issue among slaves. Just as white men compete to buy the most profitable areas of land for growing cotton, the slaves on the Randall plantation compete for the small strips of land between the slave cabins. In the same way that the Randall brothers inherit the plantation from their father, Cora inherits the vegetable patch tended first by her grandmother and then her mother. Her fierce protection of this small scrap of land demonstrates Cora's determination to hold on to the only thing in the world that she owns. By asserting her ownership, Cora defines herself as something more than someone else's property.

Violence

In *The Underground Railroad* violence is portrayed as one of the main tools in maintaining racial oppression. Violence is so much a part of everyday life for Cora that its details are mentioned almost casually. On the plantation, slaves are whipped, beaten to death and roasted on pyres. Meanwhile, in other states, runaway slaves are hung or, like Caesar, torn apart by angry mobs. Even white Americans are not immune to becoming victims of the aggression that pervades the novel, as Ethel and Martin Wells are stoned by their own townspeople when it is discovered that they have been hiding a fugitive slave. While some of the characters, such as Terrance Randall and Connelly, take a sadistic pleasure in inflicting pain on others, violence is more often portrayed as a symptom of fear. In North Carolina, one of the bloodiest states visited by Cora, the horrific incidents of violence against African Americans stem from a fear of black empowerment that borders on mass hysteria.

The abuse of power

Closely related to the theme of violence is the repeated depiction of the abuse of power. The domino effect of power abuse is particularly well illustrated on the Randall plantation. At the top of the hierarchy is Terrance Randall, who wields his power as a slave owner with a sadistic relish. Beneath him is Connelly, the Irish overseer. While Connelly is only ever a pale imitation of his master, he too exploits his power to the maximum, summoning a different slave girl to be his 'wife' each month and taking great pleasure in punishing the slaves. Below Connelly in the chain of exploitation is Moses, a black field hand who is promoted to become Connelly's enforcer due to his lack of compassion for his fellow slaves. In imitation of the overseer, Moses regularly abuses his power over the other slaves and blackmails Mabel into agreeing to sex, implying that he will rape Cora if she doesn't agree. This chain of abuse does not even stop with the ordinary slaves of the plantation. Those judged the weakest, either physically or emotionally, are banished to Hob by their fellow slaves. Meanwhile, Cora, whose unpredictable nature is feared after she destroys Blake's dog kennel, is raped by black men determined to put her in her place. This chain of abuse on the plantation illustrates the unfortunate truth that individuals who are treated as less than equal by others will usually wield what little power they have on those below them.

Language and literacy

The control of language and literacy is also shown to be a powerful tool in ensuring the continued oppression of African Americans. In South Carolina members of Cora's literacy class become frustrated with an elderly classmate, Howard, who continues to talk in "a pidgin of his lost African tongue and slave talk." While Howard's use of language seems backward to the younger members of the class, his dialect reflects the history of slavery itself. Kidnapped from many different regions of Africa, and therefore speaking different languages, first-generation slaves developed a 'half language' made up of their own native tongue and American English. Increasingly, however, their own languages were "beaten out of them over time. For simplicity, to erase their identities, to smother uprisings." Howard is, therefore, one of the few who has resisted complete colonization by retaining a scrap of his mother tongue.

Language is also used in the novel as a tool of concealment, as euphemisms are frequently used by white Americans to conceal the brutalities of racism. An avenue of mutilated corpses becomes 'the Freedom Trail', a ritual of racist propaganda followed by a murder becomes the 'Friday Festival' and the deliberate infection of black men with syphilis becomes a treatment for 'bad blood'.

Prohibiting African Americans from becoming literate is one of the most effective forms of oppression. In Georgia and North Carolina, teaching a slave to read is a crime. As a deterrent to slaves on the Randall plantation who might try to learn to read, Connelly puts out the eyes of Jacob, who he suspects of looking at words with a trace of understanding. Significantly, literacy is important to both Cora and Caesar in defining who they are. On the plantation, Caesar risks his life by regularly sneaking into the old schoolhouse to read because "if he didn't read, he was a slave." By continuing to read, he reminds himself that he is educated and his choice of reading material (*Gulliver's Travels*) reflects his hope of journeying to freedom. Cora's reading skills improve greatly as she travels along the railroad, first by taking literacy classes in South Carolina and then spending her days reading in the North Carolina attic. Her reading material is also significant as she rejects Ethel's dubiously interpreted Bible readings in favour of a story of American Indian bravery (*The Last of the Mohicans*) and the solid facts to be found in almanacs. When she reaches the Valentine farm, she spends much of her time in the library. Here she discovers that it is possible for African Americans to tell their own stories when she reads works by black writers for the first time.

History

Another subject that the novel explores is the many ways in which black history has been appropriated and distorted by white Americans. When Cora watches a white man with his face blackened playing a slave in a coon show, the moment summarizes the way in which the history of African Americans has been represented as a whole.

Cora observes that the negative portrayal of black people goes all the way back to the transcribing of the Bible. Although the holy book condemns slavery, the representation of black people as the cursed "sons of Ham" provides ideological fuel for racists. Unable to understand this discrepancy herself, Cora perceptively comes to the conclusion that the people responsible for writing the Bible deliberately got it wrong.

Elijah Landers declares that the foundations of American history are, "murder, theft, and cruelty" and it is these very aspects of the past that the Museum of Natural Wonders in South Carolina aims to gloss over. Representing scenes from Africa, a slave ship and a cotton plantation, the American History section presents a sanitised version of the African American experience, designed to be palatable to its white visitors. In this way, America erases its historical sins and covers up the damage done to African Americans in the process. While Cora has no choice but to take part in this fraudulent presentation of the history of her race, the one thing she can control is the order she plays her part in. As a living exhibit, she chooses to begin her day of roleplay on the plantation, then moves on to the slave ship, and ends the day in darkest Africa. In this small way she feels she can reverse history, journeying from slavery back to freedom.

Significantly, it is only when Cora gets to read authentic slave narratives in the Valentine farm library that she feels she is experiencing a true version of African American history for the first time. An antidote to the white rewriting of black history, they present an authentic black experience which demands to be heard.

Community

Colson Whitehead's portrayal of the slave community on the Randall plantation is particularly notable for its lack of sentimentality. While many authors would be tempted to present a black community united in their hatred of the white oppressor, the slaves in *The Underground Railroad* are far from a harmonious or supportive community. Although the slaves share moments of community spirit, such as Jockey's birthday celebrations, they are few and far between. Much more prevalent is an atmosphere of one-upmanship in which each slave is out for him or herself. When Cora is left motherless after Mabel's disappearance, no one steps forward to help her. Instead, the community make a pariah of her, banishing her to Hob. Cora's lack of status as a "stray" also means that the community turn a blind eye when she is raped by fellow slaves. Moses, a black field hand who is promoted to become Connelly's enforcer, embodies the absence of community feeling among the slaves. Selected for his lack of compassion, he gladly performs Connelly's dirty work for him and relishes abusing his power over the other slaves. Whitehead's point seems to be that the brutal and exploitative environment of slavery is unlikely to create saints. Hardship of this magnitude is more likely to make individuals seek out their own whipping boy.

While community spirit is lacking on the plantation, Cora discovers it in other surprising places. She senses it among the group of brave individuals who make up the underground railroad and also among the invisible ones who toiled to build it. She also finds contentment in the black community of Valentine farm, where everyone lives and works together for the common good. Sadly this community is destroyed by the mob of white neighbours who find the notion of black unity too frightening to tolerate. The novel suggests, however, that it is only by continuing to strive for this sense of unity that the black community will find strength. Ultimately, a celebration of the community of people who risked their lives to create and keep the underground railroad going, the novel is a reminder of what can be achieved through unity in a common cause.

Endurance

The Underground Railroad is also a celebration of the endurance of African Americans. The celebration of Jockey's birthday on the Randall plantation is much more than an excuse for a party. As the oldest slave on the plantation, Jockey has gained the respect of his fellow slaves, having survived the horrors of slavery for so long. More than anything, his birthday festivities are a celebration of physical and spiritual endurance.

Cora's character is also an inspirational example of the endurance of the human spirit. At the beginning of the novel, she is a victim not only of the white plantation owners but also of her fellow slaves. Born into slavery, she is abandoned by her mother, banished by her community to the unofficial asylum, Hob, and later raped by male slaves. Despite this victimization, however, Cora never assumes the passive demeanour of a victim. Her determination to keep the vegetable patch she inherits from her mother is demonstrated when she fearlessly destroys the usurper's dog kennel with a hatchet. Similarly, her decision to escape the plantation with Caesar is triggered when it becomes clear that Terrance Randall has singled her out as his next concubine. Although a great deal has been taken away from her, Cora remains determined to hold on to what little she has left. Ultimately defeating Ridgeway's repeated attempts to return her to the Randall plantation, she journeys on, at first with Caesar and then alone, ready to face whatever life brings.

IMAGERY

The Underground Railroad

The central motif of this novel is, of course, the underground railroad itself. Inspired by his own childhood notion of the underground railroad as a "literal subway", Whitehead decided to turn the metaphor into a physical reality. Taking full advantage of its fantastical possibilities, he portrays a variety of stations and modes of transport along the line. Some of the stations are grand, with comfortable waiting rooms and train carriages, while others are little more than roughly tunnelled-out holes with boxcars. This lack of standardization along the line emphasizes the fact that the real underground railroad wasn't a uniform entity but made up of the ad hoc efforts of many different individuals. The sweat and blood of those who have created the underground tunnel in the novel reflects the astonishing efforts of those who devoted their lives to the cause. While the real network for helping runaway slaves was only underground in the sense that it was secretive and subversive, Whitehead's literal underground railway also allows him to comment on the dark nature of racism. Cora is told by a station agent that if she looks outside as she is travelling she will "find the true face of America." Of course, all that Cora can see as she rides underground is darkness, reflecting the character of the nation as a whole.

Cotton

The significance of cotton throughout the novel is a reminder of the part this apparently innocent commodity played in the institution of slavery. Whitehead reminds the reader that cotton greatly contributed to America's prosperity during this period and the endless demand for it led to a continual need for more slaves to pick it. Wherever Cora travels she retains some connection to the cotton trade. In Georgia she grows up picking cotton to fill the coffers of white plantation owners. In South Carolina, her first employer, Mr Anderson, is also involved in the cotton trade, drawing up contracts for the industry. Significantly, one of Cora's favourite purchases when she first receives wages is a cotton dress. At first, owning the dress makes her feel as if she has come a long way from her cotton picking days. Cora's pleasure in the dress is tinged with guilt, however, as she knows that in purchasing it she is still helping to oil the wheels of the system that oppressed her.

Music

Playing music and dancing are represented as one of the few modes of free expression available to slaves in the novel. At Jockey's birthday celebrations the slaves escape from the hardship of their lives for a few hours by dancing, and in South Carolina black men and women get to know each other by dancing together at socials. Meanwhile, Jasper, the runaway slave, embodies the freedom to be found in music when he is caught by Ridgeway but refuses to stop singing, demonstrating that he might be in chains but his spirit is not beaten. Cora clearly recognizes the power of music, as she notably holds herself back from dancing when the opportunity arises. This reflects both her fear of intimacy with men and her reluctance to open the floodgates to her emotions.

The oppressive nature of white American society is illustrated by its reluctance to allow black citizens even the small freedom of music. On several occasions the enjoyment of music by black characters is curtailed by whites. At Jockey's party, the slaves' pleasure in the music is ruined when Terrance Randall gatecrashes the event and orders them to dance for his entertainment. Jasper's singing is also eventually brought to an end when Ridgeway shoots him in the face. As well as marring the joy of music, white Americans are shown appropriating black forms of musical expression to change their significance. Connelly, the white overseer, steals the work song of the plantation slaves, singing it after whipping his workers to indicate that they can go back to picking cotton. Similarly, when Cora hears a white band play in North Carolina, she realizes that they are playing traditionally black melodies but their interpretation of them makes them "bland".

American Indians

Throughout *The Underground Railroad*, the history of the American

Indian hovers in the background like a spectre. Whitehead presents the fate of American Indians as the original sin of American history, providing a blueprint for the future treatment of all other non-white races in the country. The way in which Native Americans were usurped by settlers in America is neatly reflected in Boseman's replacement of Strong, an Indian tracker employed by Ridgeway. Coveting both Strong's job and his necklace of ears, Boseman wrestles with him and finally removes him from the picture by hitting him over the head with a shovel. This nicely mirrors the tactics of those early American settlers who resorted to violence if Native Americans could not be persuaded to abandon their land in any other way. Significantly, when Boseman wears Strong's necklace, he finds that it attracts swarms of flies to his person: a problem never experienced by its original owner. Just as the homesteaders who have taken over Cherokee land in Tennessee find themselves plagued by fire and disease, Boseman finds that ownership achieved by corrupt means has its consequences. The idea that retribution must surely come is embodied in Red, the bloodthirsty American Indian who aids the underground railroad and kills Boseman.

CHARACTERS

The Underground Railroad boasts a huge cast of characters, many of whom are introduced and then never appear again. This large cast is typical of picaresque novels in which the protagonist meets many different types of individual on his travels. In this novel, however, the appearance and disappearance of characters also emphasizes the insecure nature of life as a slave. The disappearance of friends, acquaintances and even family members is a regular feature of Cora's life.

A comprehensive list of all the characters in the novel would be tediously lengthy. The following, however, is a summary of the most significant characters.

Cora

While Cora's perspective is not the only point-of-view we are privy to in the novel, the story essentially revolves around her fate. At the beginning of the novel she is a victim not only of the white plantation owners but also of her fellow slaves. Born into slavery, she is abandoned by her mother, banished by her community to the unofficial asylum, Hob, and later raped by male slaves. Despite being victimized, however, Cora never assumes the passive attitude of a victim. Her determination to keep the vegetable patch she inherits from her mother is demonstrated when she fearlessly destroys the usurper's dog kennel with a hatchet. Similarly, her decision to escape the plantation with Caesar is triggered when it becomes clear that Terrance Randall has singled her out as his next concubine. Although a great deal has been taken away from her, Cora remains determined to hold on to those things she has left.

Once she escapes, Cora's journey on the underground railroad becomes a quest for identity. While many novels centre upon the protagonist striving to discover who they really are, Cora's quest is to escape the role of chattel (represented in the x-shaped scar Terrance Randall leaves on her brow) and find a place where she is treated as a human being. Human status is, however, repeatedly denied to her. In South Carolina, she is treated like a zoological specimen in a museum and threatened with sterilization. In North Carolina, she is rendered completely invisible as she is forced to hide in a tiny attic space. Even in Indiana, where she takes refuge in a community of African Americans, autonomy is ultimately denied to her by a mob of white neighbours threatened at the prospect of black self-sufficiency.

Despite the different forms of racism she faces, Cora refuses to go along with attempts to subjugate her. This is illustrated in the hostile stares she gives to those who view her in the museum and in her refusal to agree to sterilization. Her refusal to the shaped into what white people want her to be is perhaps most neatly illustrated in the scene where Cora bluntly asks Martin's wife, Ethel, to replace her bedside Bible readings with readings from an almanac. In this request Cora thwarts Ethel's fantasies, making it clear by her interest in scientific fact that she is not the impressionable 'savage' the white woman perceives her to be.

Cora's compassion for others it demonstrated in the incident where she puts herself at risk by trying to defend Chester from his first savage beating. Most of the time, however, she keeps her feelings in check and maintains a distance between herself and others. Even in situations where she wants to express her affection to others, such as in her relationships with Caesar and Royal, she finds it very difficult to do so. The detached quality Cora possesses is largely a defence mechanism. Abandoned by her mother and raped by fellow slaves, she has little reason to trust others. Her apparent stoicism, even in the face of great suffering, also reflects the fact that, as a slave, horror has become the fabric of her everyday life.

Ultimately, Cora's quest is not only the story of an individual but also represents the historical struggle of all African Americans for freedom and equality. In this respect she is an Everywoman, encapsulating the experiences of an entire race.

Ajarry

The story of Ajarry, Cora's grandmother, is recounted in the prologue of the novel. Kidnapped from Africa, she was sold into slavery and repeatedly resold in America. Eventually ending up on the Randall plantation, Ajarry married three times and bore five children, of which only one survived to adulthood. She died of a stroke in the cotton fields.

Significantly, Ajarry never tried to escape the plantation, believing freedom to be an impossible dream. After being raped on the passage across the Atlantic, however, we learn that she tried to kill herself twice, demonstrating that she was not accepting of her fate. She also became known among her fellow slaves for fiercely guarding her vegetable plot.

By including Ajarry's story, Colson Whitehead encapsulates the slave experience through three generations of women, from capture as a free African to runaway slave in America. He also outlines the small but significant steps towards freedom that each generation makes. Ajarry never attempts to escape the plantation but passes on the determination to guard her property to her daughter, Mabel. Mabel retains the vegetable plot and escapes the plantation, only to die as she decides to return. Cora becomes the sum of both of these remarkable women, guarding her inherited plot with her life and escaping to live as free a life as she is able to find.

Mabel

The only one of Ajarry's children to live past the age of ten, Cora's mother is made of stern stuff. Determined not to die in the cotton fields, as her own mother did, she becomes the first slave to evade capture after escaping the Randall plantation. While Cora unconsciously respects her mother's memory by continuing to tend her vegetable patch and following in her fugitive slave footsteps, she cannot forgive her for abandoning her as a child. Towards the end of the novel, we learn from Mabel's narrative that she planned to return to her daughter on the plantation but died from a snake bite before she could do so. Cora never discovers her mother's real fate.

Caesar

Caesar becomes the catalyst for Cora's bid for freedom when he suggests that they should try to escape from the Randall plantation together. Unlike Cora, who was born on the plantation, Caesar was born on a farm in Virginia and his family took care of its owner, Mrs Garner. The old widow had Caesar educated and promised his family that they would be freed from slavery on her death. After she died, however, it became clear that Mrs Garner had misled them. The family were sold on and Caesar was separated from his parents. Caesar's backstory is important for, as an educated slave who was once offered the hope of freedom, he sees that a life beyond slavery is possible. Sadly Caesar meets a horrific death when a mob breaks into the South Carolina jail where he is being held and tears him to pieces.

Mrs Garner

The widow who reneges on her promise to free Caesar and his family after her death is an example of ineffectual white liberalism. While she treats the family reasonably well and ensures that Caesar is educated, she gives them the false hope of freedom without any real intention of fulfilling it. In this respect she represents the type of white American who would be insulted to be called a racist while, nevertheless, being reluctant to grant African Americans true freedom and equality.

Fletcher

A white abolitionist from Pennsylvania, Fletcher is the first agent of the underground railroad encountered by Cora and Caesar. He approaches Caesar and tells him that, if he can escape from the plantation and make the thirty mile journey to his house, he will convey him to the underground railroad. This first encounter between Fletcher and Caesar emphasizes the trust underground railroad agents and fugitive slaves had to place in one another. While Caesar faces the risk of being tricked and then punished, Fletcher places himself in an equally vulnerable position by helping a runaway slave. Later in the novel Cora and Caesar learn that Fletcher is caught for his involvement in the underground railroad.

Arnold Ridgeway

Ridgeway is the son of a blacksmith who chooses to become a slave patroller when he is fourteen rather than enter his father's profession. He progresses from this role to slave catcher and pursues his craft with an unapologetic zeal. This enthusiasm becomes an obsession when it comes to the pursuit of Cora, whose capture becomes something of a Holy Grail quest for him, following his failure to catch Cora's mother, Mabel. His dogged pursuit of Cora gives the novel the tension of a cat-and-mouse thriller.

Referring to the runaway slaves he catches as "it", Ridgeway revels in the power to stop and question any African American he meets, bringing to mind recent notorious encounters between police officers and black citizens in America. Nevertheless, he has never owned a slave himself and shows something bordering on affection for Homer, the black boy whose freedom he buys. This suggests that Ridgeway's zeal springs less from racism than a misguided belief in the righteousness of "the American spirit". Beginning with the early American settlers who displaced American Indians, Whitehead suggests that the American spirit is an empty justification for barbarity in the name of civilization. While Ridgeway's belief in it borders on religious mania, the author implies that it is an idea engrained all too deeply into the American consciousness in general.

Terrance & James Randall

Twin brothers, Terrance and James, inherit the Randall cotton plantation when their father dies. In an ingenious reflection of the American geographical divide over race before the Civil War, James inherits the northern half of the plantation while Terrance inherits the south. As in America as a whole, neither half of the plantation is exactly a utopia for its black inhabitants but living conditions on the southern half are much worse. While James Randall is just an averagely ruthless slave owner, who has his workers beaten to remind them who's boss, Terrance is a far more dangerous beast. Carrying a cane topped with a silver wolf's head to represent his predatory nature, he takes a sadistic and inventive pleasure in the torture, rape and murder of his slaves. When James dies unexpectedly, Terrance also inherits the northern half of the plantation. Aware that life on the plantation will become much worse under the rule of Terrance, who picks her out as his next sexual conquest, Cora is persuaded to risk escape. Terrance becomes obsessed with recapturing Cora, offering extravagant rewards for her return. He eventually gets his just deserts when he dies of a heart attack in a New Orleans brothel.

Connelly

Connelly is the Irish overseer of the Randall plantation and has worked there from the time of Cora's grandmother. Making the most of his power, he summons a different slave girl to be his 'wife' each month. He also relishes punishing the slaves, illustrated in the scene where he has pepper water scrubbed into the wounds of Cora and Chester after they have been whipped. Connelly is not the only morally corrupt Irish character in the novel. Fiona, the maid who betrays Cora to the night riders in North Carolina is also Irish, as is the body snatcher, Carpenter. The inclusion of these characters highlights the tensions between African Americans and Irish immigrants settling in America at this time, which largely arose out of self-interest and labour competition. Fleeing poverty and starvation in their own country, many Irish immigrants sought only to survive and had little sympathy for the plight of African Americans. A small proportion were involved in racist attacks such as the New York Draft riots in 1863 and the Memphis Massacre in 1866, as well as attempting to disrupt the activities of the underground railroad. In *The Underground Railroad*, Whitehead highlights the irony in this racism, as the Irish were also an oppressed minority in America. In North Carolina he shows black slaves being replaced by the Irish as cotton pickers, demonstrating that the new wave of immigrants are perceived as just one step up from African Americans.

Nag

Tutored from an early age by her mother in the art of pleasing white men, Nag is Connelly's preferred wife for some time. Flaunting the preferential treatment she receives in front of the other slaves, she is brought back down to earth when Connelly

tires of her and sends her to Hob. Here she redeems herself by
befriending Cora and tending to her injuries after she is beaten.

Jockey

The oldest surviving slave on the Randall plantation, Jockey
celebrates his birthday with the rest of the slaves once or even
twice a year. Jockey claims to be 101 years old but Cora knows that
he can only be half this age, as the hardship of their lives ensures
that slaves cannot possibly live much beyond fifty. The other slaves
respect Jockey for having survived the horrors of slavery for so
long. His birthday festivities are a celebration of endurance.

Chester

Cora has a soft spot for Chester, a young slave boy on the Randall
plantation. Chester, like Cora, is a "stray", as his parents were sold
off elsewhere and Cora makes a point of looking out for him,
wanting to protect him from the kind of suffering that she has
already experienced. Cora's maternal feelings towards Chester are
demonstrated when Terrance Randall beats the boy with a cane
and she instinctively steps in, shielding him with her own body.
Cora views Chester's first beating by the plantation owner as the
end of his childhood innocence. Her ultimately ineffectual defence
of him leaves her with an x-shaped scar on her temple.

Lovey

Cora's friend, Lovey, is a fun-loving girl who makes the most of
the meagre opportunities for pleasure on the plantation. When
Cora escapes from the plantation, Lovey secretly follows her. While
Cora and Caesar escape from the white men who ambush them in
the woods, however, Lovey is recaptured and suffers a lingering
death on the gallows with a large metal spike driven through her
ribs.

Ava

One of Mabel's contemporaries on the Randall plantation, Ava
does nothing to help Cora once her mother leaves, coveting her

vegetable plot, Ava is one of several unsympathetic black characters contributing to Whitehead's unsentimental portrayal of the slave community. Exploding the myth that bondage united slaves, the author illustrates the way hardship is just as likely to make individuals like Ada cruel and selfish.

Alice

Alice is favoured by the Randall brothers because of her talent in the kitchen and therefore rises towards the top of the slave hierarchy. After Mabel disappears, Alice treats Cora as a pariah and encourages others to think of her in the same way.

Moses

Another unpleasant black character, Moses is promoted from field hand to Connelly's enforcer. Selected for his complete lack of compassion, Moses gladly performs Connelly's dirty work for him and abuses his power over the other slaves. This is illustrated when Moses blackmails Mabel into agreeing to sex, implying that if she doesn't acquiesce he will rape Cora. He is also responsible for sending Cora to Hob.

Blake

When Cora is sent to Hob it is Blake, the alpha male of the slaves, who builds a dog kennel on her patch of land. Determined to reclaim what is hers, Cora destroys the dog's house with a hatchet, thereby challenging the strongest male on the plantation. Blake later takes some form of revenge by spreading lies about Cora's crazy behaviour but he, nevertheless, hands back her land. Three years after the incident, he runs away from the plantation but is caught by patrollers when his dog gives away his hiding place in a swamp. Cora doesn't describe his fate, only saying that it makes "her shiver to think about."

Edward and Pot

Two of Blake's henchmen, Edward and Pot are the slaves who rape Cora as soon as she reaches puberty. Both later meet nasty fates as Edward is hanged for trying to cheat his employer and Pot dies from complications after being bitten by a rat. While they receive their just deserts, the spectres of Edward and Pot continue to haunt Cora, making her wary of involvement with men.

Michael

Michael, the son of James Randall's coachman, is a young slave who has been taught to recite the Declaration of Independence. The irony in this novelty act is that, as a slave, he has no understanding of the concept of freedom. When the Randall brothers make a surprise appearance at Jockey's birthday celebrations, it is in the hope of seeing Michael perform his party piece. The brothers find themselves disappointed, as they learn that Connelly has beaten Michael to death without informing them.

Big Anthony

Big Anthony escapes from the Randall plantation and manages to travel 26 miles before he is found asleep in a hay loft. Once recaptured, Anthony is returned to the plantation in an iron cage to face his punishment. Terrance Randall has stocks specially constructed for the occasion, which are placed on the front lawn of the Randall house. Here Big Anthony is whipped in full view of genteel visitors having their lunch. The following day, the slaves are called from the fields to witness Big Anthony being doused with oil and roasted alive. His fate is a reminder of what lies in store for those slaves who are caught trying to escape.

Lumbly

Lumbly is an underground railroad agent with a station concealed underneath his barn. In his barn he keeps an extensive collection of iron shackles: a reminder of the bondage he helps runaway slaves to escape from.

Dr Aloysius Stevens

A short section of *The Underground Railroad* is devoted to the perspective of Dr Stevens, a white medical student. Stevens's narrative gives an account of the lucrative trade in dead bodies. As part of the terms of his fellowship, Dr Stevens is obliged to discretely admit the body snatcher, who provides the anatomy department with corpses, into the medical school. He also occasionally works for the body snatcher, helping to dig up the corpses needed for his own dissections. Stevens's commentary upon the value of corpses draws parallels between the bodysnatching trade and slavery, which both profit from the sale of human beings. As Stevens ironically observes, however, it is only in death that a black body is perceived to be just as valuable as a white one.

Carpenter and Cobb

Carpenter is the body snatcher who provides corpses to the medical school and Cobb is his accomplice. An Irishman and a racist, Carpenter concentrates on the theft of black corpses as the authorities don't ask any awkward questions when their absence is discovered. The nature of Carpenter's character is reflected in the rumour that he sold two of his children's bodies for anatomical study after they died of yellow fever.

The Andersons

Cora works for the Anderson family in South Carolina, looking after their children, cooking and cleaning. Mr Anderson spends his time drawing up contracts for the cotton industry in his law offices and Mrs Anderson does good works when she is not indisposed by her erratic mood swings. Cora is happy working for the family and, when she is abruptly moved on to work in the museum, misses their children. When she sees Maisie Anderson staring at her in the museum, however, Cora gives the little girl the "evil eye" as she realizes that the Andersons viewed her as a disposable commodity.

Miss Lucy

Cora at first sees Miss Lucy, the proctor of her dormitory in South Carolina, as something of a guardian angel. Civil and encouraging, Miss Lucy appears to want the best for her charges, ensuring they become literate and finding them employment Cora sees Miss

Lucy's true colours, however, when the proctor tries to coerce her into sterilization. Miss Lucy embodies one of the most insidious forms of racism. While condemning slavery and appearing to desire freedom and equality for her girls, she aims to control and limit that freedom to a level that she feels comfortable with.

Sam

Sam, the young station agent of South Carolina, has a station hidden under his barn. While he is prepared to risk his life to help runaway slaves, he is initially blind to the racism underlying the organization of his home state. Sam's job in a saloon comes in handy as it is in the bar that he hears about the government's syphilis research program and learns of Ridgeway's appearance in South Carolina. He pays the price for helping Cora to safety when his house is set alight but survives the fire and continues to work for the underground railroad. He later turns up at Valentine's farm, Indiana, and gives Cora the good news that Terrance Randall has died.

Gertrude

During her stay in South Carolina, Cora sees Gertrude, a young black woman, running distressed and half-naked through the town. Cora initially assumes that when Gertrude cries that her babies are being taken, she is reliving past trauma from her life as a slave. She later realizes, however, that Gertrude's cries of distress relate to the state's sterilization program for black women. Miss Lucy tells Cora that, following the incident, Gertrude was relocated to dormitory 40: the quarters reserved for women with "nervous disorders", who can be routinely sterilized without giving their consent. The incident causes Cora to conclude that the state's paternalistic encouragement of sterilization for black women is actually a case of racist eugenics.

Martin Wells

Martin Wells inherits a map of the underground railroad from his father and honours his promise to carry on his father's work by helping runaway slaves to reach the free states. Just prior to his first meeting with Cora, however, he decides that he will have to give up his role as a station agent, as the work has become too dangerous in the white supremacist state of North Carolina. When he discovers Cora waiting at the abandoned station, Martin has little choice but to hide her in his home. His fears of discovery are shown to be well-founded when his townspeople discover that he and his wife have been concealing a runaway slave and stone them.

Ethel Wells

Martin's wife, Ethel, disapproves of her husband's involvement in the underground railroad and is displeased at Cora's arrival. An example of an unchristian Christian, Ethel interprets scripture in a way that supports her racist beliefs. When Cora falls ill, we begin to reassess Ethel's character as she nurses her patient and reads to her from the Bible. Soon it becomes clear, however, that Ethel sees Cora's illness as an opportunity to bring God to the savages.

In the short section of the novel written from Ethel's perspective we learn that her distorted views on race have been inherited from her father. As a child she is initially unprejudiced and her best friend, Jasmine, is black. Although Jasmine is the daughter of her father's house slave, Felice, Ethel thinks of her as family – a belief supported by the fact that her father visits Felice's bedroom each night. She is forced to view Jasmine through different eyes, however, when her father stops them playing together, informing her that African Americans are the "descendants of cursed, black Ham". When Felice becomes too ill to be of use in the house or the bedroom, she is sold on, while teenage Jasmine is left to perform all her mother's duties. Aware that her father has now started to visit her old playmate at night, Ethel displaces her feelings of revulsion onto Jasmine. Later, when Jasmine has a son who is clearly Ethel's half-brother, she ignores them both, choosing not to acknowledge her father's depravity and hypocrisy. Ethel's backstory suggests that racism is not a natural trait but one that is learned from others.

In the end, Ethel's belief that Cora will bring danger to her house proves to be true. When they receive an unexpected visit from the night riders Ethel betrays her husband in an attempt to save herself. Nevertheless, her act of disloyalty does not prevent her from being stoned by the crowd in the park.

Fiona

Fiona is the young Irish maid who works for the Wells family and betrays Cora's presence to the night riders. Cora is aware that Fiona is unhappy with her lot, as she hears her swearing and complaining while she is hiding in the attic. While Fiona's situation is several steps up from that of a slave, we learn that she lives in the impoverished ghetto of Irishtown in which the Irish immigrants are segregated.

Homer

One of the strangest characters in the novel, Homer is the black boy of about ten years old who drives Ridgeway's wagon and keeps his business accounts. Always dressed in a suit and stovepipe, Homer takes great pride in his appearance and has the air of an old man. Although once a slave himself, he shows no empathy for the runaway slaves he helps to recapture.

The relationship between Homer and his master, Ridgeway, is an enigmatic one. Claiming to see a fellow spirit in the black boy, Ridgeway, who isn't known for his compassion towards slaves, buys Homer and immediately draws up his emancipation papers. He also makes sure the boy receives an education. Despite being given his freedom, however, Homer chooses to stay with Ridgeway and even manacles himself to the wagon every night, as this is the only way he can sleep soundly. Homer's apparent determination to remain enslaved reveals both fear of the unknown and a realization that being a 'free black' is unlikely to provide either freedom or equality.

Jasper

A runaway slave caught by Ridgeway, Jasper annoys the slave catcher by continually singing on the journey, even though he has a terrible voice. Jasper's repeated singing of hymns and refusal to accept food from Ridgeway demonstrates an inner strength that will not be quashed. Eventually, Ridgeway shoots Jasper in the face to silence him, thereby foregoing the reward he would have collected for him. While this incident is horrifying it represents a spiritual and moral victory for Jasper.

Boseman

Ridgeway's colleague, Boseman, is a sadistic brute, known for wearing a necklace of human ears. The necklace previously belonged to an American Indian who formerly worked with Ridgeway until they had a dispute. Boseman's corrupt nature is nicely illustrated by the fact that flies swarm around the necklace when he wears it, although they apparently never bothered its previous owner. Boseman attempts to rape Cora after helping to recapture her but Ridgeway catches him in the act and prevents it.

Royal

Royal is a freeborn black man and a conductor on the underground railroad. Cora first meets him when he rescues her from Ridgeway. His actions are later to save her a second time, as he shows her the location of the underground railroad's ghost tunnel. Cora develops feelings for Royal during her stay on the Valentine farm and, when he is killed in the white raid, she regrets failing to tell him that she loved him.

Red

Red is an American Indian associate of Royal who dedicated himself to the cause of the underground railroad after his wife and children were killed by regulators. Unlike Royal, however, who refrains from using violence, Red is fuelled by a bloodthirsty desire for revenge and it is he who kills Boseman. His character is representative of those American Indians who supported the underground railroad in real life, presumably seeing parallels between the oppression of their own people and that of African Americans.

John Valentine

The owner of Valentine farm, John Valentine, is a wealthy free black. His unusually light skin colour has greatly contributed to his success, as white people make the assumption that he is one of them. He uses his apparent whiteness to help other black people, setting up the farm as an office for the underground railroad, creating a self-sufficient black community and offering refuge to runaway slaves.

Molly

Cora develops a bond with Molly, a ten-year-old girl who lives with her mother, Sybil, on the Valentine farm. As with Cora's relationship with Chester, her affection for Molly highlights her maternal instincts and her attraction to childhood innocence. Observing Molly's close bond with Sybil also prompts Cora to mourn the relationship she never had the chance to develop with her own mother.

Mingo

Mingo is one of the few residents of Valentine farm who believes that runaway slaves should not be given shelter there. He argues that, by giving refuge to slaves, they risk incurring the wrath of the white community. A former slave himself, Mingo has purchased the freedom of himself, his wife and his children. He is an example of the type of individual who wants freedom for himself and his loved ones but is not prepared to fight for those still enslaved. There is more than a suggestion that Mingo is the informant who brings Arnold Ridgeway to the farm.

Elijah Lander

Elijah is one of the few mixed race characters in the novel. Significantly, he is not the offspring of an illicit or unequal relationship but the legitimate son of a rich white lawyer and his black wife. Elijah's biracial identity gives him influence among whites and blacks alike. A charismatic speaker with a brilliant mind, he gives speeches on racial equality, reminiscent of those made by Martin Luther King before his assassination in the 1960s. Elijah also meets a violent end when he is shot while giving a rousing speech at the Valentine farm. Nevertheless, his presence in the novel seems to offer hope for the future.

LOCATIONS

Lumbly, the station agent, tells Cora that her journey on the underground railroad will enable her to, "see the breadth of the country before you reach your final stop." This comment is somewhat ironic as nothing but darkness can be seen from the railroad track. Once Cora emerges at each stop, however, she does experience almost everything that the country has to offer an African American. Each location has its own customs and laws, reflecting the nation's attitudes towards slavery and the race question, not only across different states but across history. While some states are significantly worse than others, none of them offer African Americans complete freedom or equality and Cora's quest continues beyond the conclusion of the novel.

Georgia

Cora's story begins on the Randall cotton plantation in the southern state of Georgia. Here slaves suffer great hardship and savage punishments without any prospect of freedom, unless they are prepared to risk their lives attempting to escape. Even within the plantation, however, there are varying degrees of suffering. Whitehead ingeniously splits ownership of the estate between the twin brothers, James and Terrance, with the less brutal brother overseeing the northern half, while Terrance, the utter sadist, rules over the south. In this way the author creates a microcosm of America, where slavery is institutionalized in the South but not practiced in the free states of the North. Significantly, however, the author does not present James Randall as a completely benign slave owner or his half of the plantation as a utopia. Slaves are still beaten on the northern half of the estate and Master James gives a free hand to Connelly, the overseer, who is a racist brute. In this way Whitehead makes the point that, while the free states of the North offered an improved life for African Americans, they were not the Promised Land many slaves envisioned.

The northern half of the plantation is further segregated with the creation of Hob: the slave quarters to which the "wretched" are banished. As well as those who have been orphaned by slavery, like Cora, the residents of Hob are those women who bear visible physical or psychological scars from their lives as slaves. They include women who have lost their wits after the death of all their children, women who are physically disabled from one beating too many, a woman who chooses to be mute because of the horrors she has witnessed and another who cannot talk as her tongue was cut out by a previous owner. The walls of Hob protect both the white plantation owners and the other slaves from being reminded of the different ways that slavery can destroy a human being. Ironically, they also provide a kind of protection for its residents, as Hob women are less likely to be sexually preyed upon by men of either colour.

South Carolina

Cora's first stop on the underground railroad is South Carolina and, when she first arrives here, she feels that her life of freedom has begun. In this state, slavery does not exist and the government runs programs to help house black citizens and find them work. Working conditions are much better here and literacy is actively encouraged. It slowly becomes clear, however, that things are not as ideal as they seem. While seeming to offer freedom to its black residents, the state seeks to limit and control that freedom in almost every area. Although Cora and Caesar are no longer slaves, they are still officially owned by the government. Their new identity papers, while appearing to protect them from recapture, also dictate the names by which they will be known. They are paid for their work, but prices for basics such as food and accommodation are so inflated that there is no danger of them ever becoming wealthy. Black men become the subjects of medical research into syphilis without their knowledge or consent and black women are coerced into sterilization. Meanwhile, in the Museum of Natural Wonders where Cora is sent to work, a sanitized version of American history is displayed, seeking to gloss over the brutalities of slavery.

During her time in South Carolina, Cora reluctantly comes to the conclusion that the black freedom being peddled here is an illusion. While acknowledging that slavery is an inhumane institution, the state still finds the idea of racial equality a threat and is only prepared to consider emancipation if the black population can be kept at a 'manageable' level. For those who do not comply there is dormitory number 40, the quarters reserved for the mentally ill. Cora observes that dormitory 40 is the equivalent of Hob on the plantation. Women are banished there for failing to conform and are then perceived as less than human. Once in this dormitory their fates can be decided without having to worry about the inconvenient issue of human rights. While at first seeming a million miles away from Georgia in its attitudes to race, Cora concludes that in coming to South Carolina, "They had not travelled very far at all."

North Carolina

When Cora reaches North Carolina she finds the station closed and its agent, Martin Wells, completely unprepared for her arrival. On the way to the station agent's home there are more unwelcoming omens as they follow the Freedom Trail into town: a tree-lined avenue festooned with black corpses. Cora discovers that, while slavery has been abolished in North Carolina, so has the black population. Its citizens have solved 'the colored question' by making it an entirely white state. Night riders patrol the state, keeping the population safe from the presence of African Americans, while Irish immigrants harvest the cotton once picked by black slaves.

Cora is trapped in North Carolina for several months, as Martin is unable to get word to any of his railroad connections without endangering the life of himself, his wife and Cora. Forced to make herself invisible, even to the Wells's maid, she hides in a tiny concealed nook in the attic. The similarities between her situation and that of Anne Frank are no accident, as the hellish state has much in common with Nazi Germany. The 'Friday Festival' that Cora witnesses through a hole in the attic wall is reminiscent of Nazi propaganda against the Jews, including the ridiculing and dehumanizing of African Americans in a coon show. The evening's entertainment is then concluded with a spectacle of ethnic cleansing: the public hanging of a fugitive slave girl.

Tennessee

When Ridgeway recaptures Cora, they travel through Tennessee on his wagon. On the journey Ridgeway points out that they are travelling through land which used to belong to American Indians before they were pushed out by white settlers. The landscape of Tennessee has a surreal, almost Biblical flavour, as they pass through a charred wasteland, devastated by a fire that has burned out of control. On reaching the limits of the fire's radius, they then travel past a series of towns overcome by yellow fever. The disasters that have befallen the state have the unmistakable quality of plagues sent by God: a theory that Boseman seems to buy into when he suggests that the settlers, left homeless by the fire, must have done something to incur God's wrath. Significantly both disasters have occurred as a direct result of the citizens' actions (the fire is started by homesteaders burning scrub and the yellow fever arrived on the boats bringing slaves from the West Indies). Tennessee, therefore, bears all the signs of a state suffering retribution for its oppression of other races. While Cora initially believes that Tennessee is "cursed", however, she comes to the conclusion that it is simply the random hand of fate, as "there is no earthly justice." Readers are left to make up their own minds.

Indiana

Of all the American states she visits in the novel, Cora comes closest to freedom in Indiana. Here she joins a largely harmonious black community on the Valentine farm. Cora is happy here, where she has access to books and works for the benefit of herself and the community. The divisions within the residents over the future of the farm, however, provide a hint of the trouble that is to come. Some are happy to shelter fugitive slaves, while others want the community to consist of only free blacks, feeling that this will provide their best chance of flourishing without the interference of whites. Yet another faction feels that, as Indiana still shares a border with slave states, their community should relocate further west where a number of black towns have emerged. In the end, concerns that Valentine farm is too good to be true prove well-founded. Threatened by the presence of a self-sufficient black community in their vicinity, white residents of the nearby towns invade the farm, killing many of its residents.

DISCUSSION QUESTIONS

1/ *The Underground Railroad* includes the narratives of three generations of women: Ajarry, Mabel and Cora. What do these characters have in common and how do they differ? Does the difference in their fates suggest progress down the generations?

2/ How did you feel about Mabel's decision to run away from the Randall plantation without her daughter? Is Cora's hatred of her mother justified?

3/ Discuss the way Cora is treated by the other slaves on the Randall plantation after she is abandoned by her mother. Did this negative portrayal of the black community surprise you? What point do you think the author is making? Are there any positive representations of community in the novel?

4/ Although Cora is victimized by others she never behaves like a victim. Discuss the ways in which she fights against the different types of oppression she encounters.

5/ Cora's story is told through a third-person narrator. Why do you think the author chose a third-person narrative for his subject matter? What impact does it have on the tone of the novel? Did the narrative work for you or would you have preferred a first-person narration?

6/ Discuss the different forms of racism Cora encounters in the American states she passes through. What is this prejudice driven by? Which state, in your opinion, was the worst in its violation of human rights?

7/ While Cora's perspective dominates, *The Underground Railroad* includes narratives from the point-of-view of a range of other characters. Why do you think the author includes the stories of relatively minor characters such as Dr Stevens and Ethel Wells? Did they add anything to the novel?

8/ The novel introduces a dazzling array of characters, many of whom appear only briefly. Why do you think the author introduces characters only to have them disappear shortly afterwards? Did you appreciate the large cast of characters or find it confusing?

9/ Discuss the author's use of deliberate anachronisms and magic realism in his story. How do these elements allow the author to express things that could not be conveyed in a strictly realist novel? How did you feel about the combination of realism and fantasy? Is it appropriate for Whitehead's subject matter?

10/ Discuss the way in which the control of language and literacy is shown to be a powerful tool in maintaining the oppression of African Americans.

11/ Ridgeway's guiding philosophy is a belief in "the American spirit". What does he mean by this? How does his belief relate to the references to American Indians in the novel?

12/ One of Cora's jobs in South Carolina is to work as a live exhibit in the Museum of Natural Wonders. What does this experience say about America's attitude to its national history?

13/ In the paternalistic state of South Carolina, Cora discovers that black women are being sterilized without their consent, while black men are the unwitting subjects of research into syphilis. Did it surprise you that these fictional incidents were based on historical fact? Is state control of population numbers ever ethically acceptable?

14/ Discuss the parallels the novel draws between Cora's experience in North Carolina and the regime of Nazi Germany. Can you think of more recent events which also bear a similarity to the atmosphere of racial hatred and fear Cora finds in North Carolina?

15/ By the closing pages of the novel Cora still has a long way to travel before she reaches freedom. Did you interpret the ending in an optimistic light?

16/ In what way does Cora's journey represent the experiences of an entire race?

17/ While Whitehead's novel is set over a century and a half ago, we still find ourselves in an era where black Americans feel the need to remind society that 'Black Lives Matter'. How much progress have we made in the achievement of racial equality?

18/ Have you read any other fictional or factual books about African American slavery? If so, do you feel that *The Underground Railroad* makes a new and significant contribution to this canon of work? Do you feel that the novel gave you a deeper understanding of the slave experience?

QUIZ QUESTIONS

1/ What is the name of the slave quarters Cora finds herself banished to after her mother disappears?

2/ What does Mabel take with her when she escapes from the Randall plantation?

3/ How does Mabel die?

4/ What is the slave boy, Michael, famous for?

5/ What promise does Caesar's former owner, Mrs Garner, fail to keep?

6/ Which three aspects of African American history does Cora have to represent in the Museum of Natural Wonders?

7/ In South Carolina a state program experiments on unwitting black men to research which disease?

8/ What is the name of the tree-lined avenue festooned with mutilated black corpses?

9/ Where does Cora have to hide when she reaches North Carolina?

10/ In North Carolina who reveals Cora's presence to the night riders?

11/ What does Ridgeway's colleague, Boseman, wear around his neck?

12/ What type of book does Royal buy for Cora?

QUIZ ANSWERS

1/ Hob

2/ The yams she has grown in her vegetable plot

3/ She is bitten by a snake while hiding in a swamp

4/ Reciting the Declaration of Independence

5/ To grant Caesar and his family freedom when she dies

6/ Darkest Africa, life on a slave ship and life on a plantation

7/ Syphilis

8/ The Freedom Trail

9/ In a tiny nook of the station agent's attic

10/ The Irish maid, Fiona

11/ A necklace of ears

12/ An up-to-date almanac

FURTHER READING

Beloved by Toni Morrison

Homegoing by Yaa Gyasi

The Known World by Edward P. Jones

The Sellout by Paul Beatty

Incidents in the Life of a Slave Girl by Harriet Jacobs

Twelve Years a Slave by Solomon Northup

Gulliver's Travels by Johnathan Swift

One Hundred Years of Solitude by Gabriel Garcia Marquez

BIBLIOGRAPHY

Colson Whitehead. *The Underground Railroad*, Doubleday, 2016

Ron Charles. 'Oprah's Book Club Pick: *The Underground Railroad* by Colson Whitehead.' *The Washington Post*, 2 August 2016

Michelle Dean. 'Colson Whitehead: 'My agent said: Oprah. I said: Shut the front door.' *The Guardian*, 17 August 2016

Andray Domise. 'Review: Colson Whitehead's *The Underground Railroad* is a powerful reimagining of American history.' *The Globe and Mail*, 12 August 2016

Michiko Kaktani. 'Review: 'Underground Railroad' Lays Bare Horrors of Slavery and its Toxic Legacy.' *The New York Times*, 2 August 2016

Laura Miller. 'Practicing art with liberty and joy.' *The Slate Book Review*, 10 August 2016

Jennifer Schuessler. 'Colson Whitehead on slavery, success and writing the novel that really scared him.' *The New York Times*, 2 August 2016

Juan Gabriel Vasquez. 'In Colson Whitehead's latest, the Underground Railroad is more than a metaphor.' *The New York Times*, 5 August 2016

FURTHER TITLES IN THIS SERIES

The Book Thief (Markus Zusak): A Guide for Book Clubs

The Fault in Our Stars (John Green): A Guide for Book Clubs

Frankenstein (Mary Shelley): A Guide for Book Clubs

The Girl on the Train (Paula Hawkins): A Guide for Book Clubs

Go Set a Watchman (Harper Lee): A Guide for Readers

A God in Ruins (Kate Atkinson): A Guide for Book Clubs

The Goldfinch (Donna Tartt): A Guide for Book Clubs

Gone Girl (Gillian Flynn): A Guide for Book Clubs

The Great Gatsby (F. Scott Fitzgerald): A Guide for Book Clubs

The Grownup (Gillian Flynn): A Guide for Book Clubs

The Guernsey Literary and Potato Peel Pie Society (Mary Ann Shaffer & Annie Burrows): A Guide for Book Clubs

The Heart Goes Last (Margaret Atwood): A Guide for Book Clubs

The Husband's Secret (Liane Moriarty): A Guide for Book Clubs

I Know Why the Caged Bird Sings (Maya Angelou): A Guide for Book Clubs

The Light between Oceans (M.L. Stedman): A Guide for Book Clubs

My Brilliant Friend (Elena Ferrante): A Guide for Book Clubs

My Name is Lucy Barton (Elizabeth Strout): A Guide for Book Clubs

The Narrow Road to the Deep North (Richard Flanagan): A Guide for Book Clubs

The Paying Guests (Sarah Waters): A Guide for Book Clubs

The Secret History (Donna Tartt): A Guide for Book Clubs

The Storied Life of A.J. Fikry (Gabrielle Zevin): A Guide for Book Clubs

The Sympathizer (Viet Thanh Nguyen): A Guide for Book Clubs

ABOUT THE AUTHOR

Kathryn Cope graduated in English Literature from Manchester University and obtained her master's degree in contemporary fiction from the University of York. She is a reviewer and author of The Reading Room Book Group Guides. She lives in the Peak District with her husband and son.

www.amazon.com/author/kathryncope

48669000R00039

Made in the USA
Middletown, DE
24 September 2017